Reset of the Mindset

Alinging your thoughts for guidance and purpose

By

Mary Braham

12808 West Airport Blvd Suite 270M Sugar Land, TX 77478, Unites States

https://www.theempirepublishers.com/

Our books may be purchased in bulk for promotional, educational, or business use.

Please contact The Empire Publishers at +1 844 636-4579, or by email at support@theempirepublishers.com

First Edition December 2024

Dedication

To my Sonshine, Rodrekus Braham

You were the light when I have darkness, I will love you for eternity. Continue to always shine brightly and chase your dreams, knowing that my love will be with you every step of the way. Thank you for being my motivation.

 In Loving memory of Dorothy Shuree Allen 12/26/1976 – 10/16/1993

About the Author

As a Certified Spiritual Coach, I delve deeply into the emotional and spiritual aspects of personal growth. My mission is to help clients discover their core values, strengths, and passions, guiding them to align their lives with their true purpose. I've seen firsthand the transformative impact of embracing one's authentic self, and that drives my passion for this work. Whether through one-on-one coaching or group workshops, I am committed to providing a safe and supportive space where individuals can explore their dreams, challenges, and aspirations.

In addition to my coaching practice, I am also an author. Writing has always been a deeply fulfilling passion for me, and through my books, I aim to offer insights and practical strategies that empower readers to embrace their unique journeys. I believe storytelling is a powerful way to foster connection and understanding, and my goal is to inspire others to write their own stories of empowerment, growth, and success.

Table of Contents

Chapter 1
The Transformative Power of a Renewed Mindset

Our mindset is the invisible force that shapes our lives, guiding our choices, our perspective, and ultimately, our destiny. As followers of the Highest Most, we are called to live with purpose and fulfillment, yet often find ourselves feeling stuck, unsure, or overwhelmed by the circumstances around us. In these moments, it's crucial to understand that the way we think—our mindset—holds the key to unlocking the abundant life God has planned for us. I am here to tell you through divine guidance that I went through what I call a reset of the mindset. It completely changed my life. I truly began to understand the true meaning of "knock, and the door will be opened unto you, and seek me and ye shall find me." Seeking is to go within. To go within is to seek. When the door opens, you will begin to see that everything is mindset. It is truly possible no matter who or what you are, or what you have done. The saying "come as you are" is very true. You being the most important word in the saying, because you have to quiet the mind so that you may begin to know your purpose. God can't reach you through anger, overthinking, unforgiveness, etc. God doesn't connect with you through negative emotions. The mind has to be quiet. This is my journey, and as I entered into this journey, I knew right away that I would go a very different route. I learned things more deeply and intensely, a wonderful experience. This book is to help you Bloom Boldly Mindfully. The process that I experienced can help you change your life without changing or getting ready, or getting rid of. This process is about having divine guidance.

In the sacred quiet of our inner world, our thoughts shape the very essence of our being. The heart, often viewed as the seat of emotions, is also a profound reservoir of our deepest beliefs and aspirations. When we cultivate thoughts of love, compassion, and gratitude, we align ourselves with the divine flow of the universe. Changing the way we think can ultimately lead to peace. Peace is needed for true guidance, so that you may learn to flow.

Each thought is a seed, planted in the fertile ground of the heart, nurturing the garden of our lives. If we dwell upon negativity, fear, or doubt, we may find ourselves lost in shadows. Conversely, when we embrace positivity and hope, we illuminate our path and inspire those around us.

Let us, therefore, be mindful of what we nurture within. For in the sacred dance between thought and spirit, we have the power to transform ourselves and, in turn, the world around us. As we think, so we become; let our hearts be filled with light, guiding us toward a destiny rich with purpose and love.

This book is designed to be a guide for anyone seeking to reset their mindset and experience true transformation through the renewing of their mind. Transformation is not just about positive thinking or self-help strategies; it's about aligning your thoughts with God's truth and trusting in His guidance. Through practical steps, biblical wisdom, and powerful stories of spiritual transformation, this book aims to show you how to renew your mind and live the fulfilling, abundant life that God promises.

The journey we will embark on in these pages is one of mind renewal—a journey of exchanging negative, limiting thoughts for ones that are empowered by faith, hope, and action in the Lord. This transformation involves four key elements: faith, acceptance, forgiveness, and action.

Faith is the foundation of personal transformation. It is faith that opens our hearts to the possibilities of change, even when the circumstances seem impossible. Faith is not just about believing in God's power; it's about trusting in His ability to do the impossible in our lives. As we cultivate faith in our hearts, our mindset shifts, and we start to approach each day with the mindset of possibility, knowing that God has already gone before us and made a way. It can be hard to have faith when everything in your life seems to never go as you would like. We all have those experiences, but the key is to remember that it's not just you - some have had and have things much worse. It wasn't and it isn't to hurt you; it's to build you. But your story is your story - what you went through, good or bad, it is your story. And when you realize why, then everything will have been worth it. The pain can lead to purpose. So things sometimes have to not work in order to work. You will never have more than you can bear, even if that means you ended up crashing. Things have to end, so that you may bloom.

Acceptance is the recognition of where we are right now, without self-judgment or condemnation. It's a choice to see our situation as it is, while still believing that God is leading us toward something better. True transformation happens when we accept our current reality while still trusting in God's perfect plan and timing for our lives. No matter what you have been through in life, you must accept it and understand that it was only part of your story, your experiences. It had to come from the ones we love and trusted the most, or it would not be pain, and you can't experience love without pain. Do not be a victim to what someone else did to you; accept it, grow from it, and leave it in the past.

Forgiveness is a powerful and transformative force, allowing us to let go of the heavy weight of resentment and anger, and giving ourselves the freedom to move forward in Christ. By forgiving others and ourselves, we align ourselves with God's grace and love, making room for peace, joy, and the possibility of real spiritual transformation. Some things can be very hard to forgive, but it's not for them; it's for you. Unforgiveness is like a dark cloud over the heart and makes it hard for the mind's eye, also known as the third eye, to see, and the heart to feel. For God to give us the desires of our heart, it has to be felt from the heart, and there is no way you can fool the heart.

Finally, transformation requires action. Faith without deeds is dead. God doesn't just call us to envision a transformed life; He calls us to walk toward it, trusting in His guidance and empowerment along the way. As we take steps of faith, we become the living testament of the faith we profess, and God uses our obedience to bring about His purposes. Faith is believing without seeing, so no matter what your life looks like, it's about to change. You have to believe that at this very moment, so that the heart can feel. If things are falling apart, let them fall; it has to in order to come together. What I had planned for myself was much greater than I ever imagined.

Throughout this book, you will be challenged to break free from the patterns of fear, insecurity, and complacency that have held you back. Together, we will explore how you can embrace God's promises, transform your thinking, and move forward in faith to live the fulfilling life destined for you. Get ready to experience the transformative power of a renewed mindset.

Chapter 2
Faith as the Spiritual Foundation

Faith is the bedrock of this process. When everything around us seems uncertain or out of place, faith steadies our hearts and minds, allowing us to press forward. It's a divine force that enables us to perceive the unseen, believe in the impossible, and trust that transformation starts within.

In this chapter, we will explore the profound importance of faith, both in yourself and in a higher power, and how it plays a crucial role in shifting your mindset and overcoming life's tribulations. We will delve into why faith is essential for personal transformation, how it fuels positive change, and share spiritual exercises to help you build and strengthen your belief, even in the face of adversity.

Defining Faith in Yourself and a Higher Calling

At its core, faith is the confident assurance that what we hope for will come to pass, even if we can't yet see it. It's believing in the unseen and trusting in God's divine plan, even when the path ahead is shrouded in mystery. The Bible reminds us in Hebrews 11:1 that "faith is the substance of things hoped for, the evidence of things not seen." Faith in yourself is the belief that, despite your imperfections and failures, you are capable of becoming the spiritual being God created you to be. It's having confidence in your innate abilities, the courage to pursue your heavenly-inspired dreams, and the trust that you can grow and evolve with God's sacred guidance.

Faith in God, however, takes this belief to an even deeper, more sacred level. It's the trust that God is in sovereign control of your life and that by being faithful to fulfill eternal promises, even when your current reality doesn't seem to match the vision in your heart. Faith in God is the assurance that God is with you through every trial and every triumph, that Gods divine wisdom will guide you, and boundless power will enable you to overcome every obstacle in your path.

When these two types of faith—faith in yourself and faith in God—work together, they create a powerful, spiritual force for transformation. Faith in God strengthens your belief in yourself, while faith in yourself opens your heart to receive God's bountiful blessings. The two are inseparable, working in harmonious tandem to create the life your Creator has destined for you.

Why Faith is Crucial for Spiritual Mindset Change

Faith is not just about what you believe; it's about how those beliefs influence your thoughts, actions, and decisions. When you cultivate faith, you begin to align your mindset with the eternal truth of God's Word. You start to see challenges as sacred opportunities, not obstacles, and you believe that, with God's divine help, you can navigate through life's spiritual storms.

Changing your mindset requires faith because it demands that you move beyond what your eyes can see into what your heart knows to be true. The journey of personal transformation begins in the mind. Romans 12:2 tells us, "Do not conform to the pattern of this world, but be transformed by the renewing of your mind." This renewal of the mind is a shift from a limited, negative perspective to one filled with the hope and promise of God's eternal truth.

Faith is perceiving the unseen—the divine possibility that lies beyond your current circumstances. It's believing in a future that looks different from your present reality, and trusting that God's plans for you are greater than any challenge you face. When you reset your mindset and align your thoughts with the sacred life you want to live, you begin to attract what you need. You have to see it in your heart before you see it with your eyes.

Life will test your faith again and again. These challenges are not meant to break you but to refine and strengthen you. Every failure, every setback, every trial is a lesson—a stepping stone to spiritual growth. As you face difficulties, your faith is tested, and the more you trust God through each trial, the stronger your belief becomes.

You may not pass every test on the first try, but that's part of the process. The same test may appear repeatedly until you learn to trust God fully. And when you do pass that test, you'll realize that the struggle was part of the divine preparation for the breakthrough that was always meant for you.

Forgiveness and Faith: The Sacred Connection

An essential part of faith is forgiveness. Faith and forgiveness are intricately connected, and unforgiveness can block the blessings and transformation that God wants to bring into your life. Holding on to resentment is like carrying a weight that prevents you from moving forward. But when you forgive, you free yourself from that burden, allowing your heart and mind to be open to God's sacred work in your life.

Jesus' words in Matthew 6:14-15 make it clear: "For if you forgive other people when they sin against you, your heavenly Father will also forgive you. But if you do not forgive others their sins, your Father will not forgive your sins." Forgiveness is not optional—it's essential for spiritual growth and personal freedom. It's not just about letting others off the hook; it's about releasing the pain, anger, and bitterness that keep you stuck in the past.

Forgiveness can be difficult, especially when the wounds run deep. But it is through forgiving others that we begin to heal, and it is through God's forgiveness of us that we find the strength to forgive. Sometimes, the hardest person to forgive is ourselves, and yet, until we do, we will not fully experience the freedom that comes from God's divine grace.

Exercises to Strengthen Belief in Positive Outcomes Despite Challenging Circumstances

Building and maintaining faith, especially when life feels overwhelming, is not something that happens overnight. It takes intention, practice, and unwavering commitment. Below are some practical, spiritual exercises to help strengthen your belief in positive outcomes, even in difficult times:

Visualize the Heavenly Future You Desire: Take time each day to visualize the sacred life you want to live. See yourself succeeding in your divine calling, mending relationships, or overcoming obstacles. Picture yourself walking in the fullness of God's eternal promises. When you align your heart with God's vision for your life, you begin to see things differently, and your faith grows.

Write Out Your Faith Confessions: Write down affirmations based on God's Word. Declare His promises over your life. For example, "I am more than a conqueror through Christ who strengthens me" (Romans 8:37), or "I can do all things through Christ who strengthens me" (Philippians 4:13). Speak these sacred truths out loud each day, allowing them to sink deep into your spirit.

Keep a Faith Journal: Document your journey of faith. Write about the challenges you face, but also record the victories, no matter how small. Reflect on how God has been faithful in the past, and use those reminders as fuel for your faith. This journal will be a testimony to God's power and His faithfulness in your life.

Practice Forgiveness Daily: Take a moment each day to examine your heart. Are there areas where you are holding on to resentment? Pray for the strength to forgive, and ask God to help you release any bitterness or unforgiveness. Forgiveness is a choice, and as you choose to forgive, you align yourself with God's grace and open the door for His blessings to flow freely into your life.

Step Out in Faith: Faith without action is dead (James 2:26). Take one small step toward the sacred life you envision. It could be as simple as applying for a new job, reaching out to someone you need to reconcile with, or beginning a new spiritual habit. Every action you take in faith is a declaration that you believe God will provide the strength and resources to make it happen.

Conclusion: Faith as the Key to Spiritual Transformation

Faith is the foundation of every transformation. It is the trust in God's goodness, the belief that He is working in your life, and the assurance that your dreams can become reality when you align your mind and heart with His divine will. By strengthening your faith in yourself and in God, you open the door to limitless spiritual possibilities.

As you face life's challenges, remember that faith is not about what you see with your eyes, but about what you believe with your heart. Hold fast to your faith, take action, and trust that God is shaping you for something greater. The journey of transformation is not always easy, but with faith, you will rise above every spiritual storm and step into the sacred life you were created to live.

Chapter 3
Cultivating Spiritual Focus and Prioritization

In this fast-paced, distraction-filled world, it can be a constant struggle to maintain spiritual focus and ensure our daily actions are aligned with God's greater purpose for our lives. Whether it's the pressures of work, family obligations, or the relentless pull of worldly temptations, it's easy to feel overwhelmed and lose sight of our true calling. Yet, the ability to balance our earthly responsibilities while staying committed to the transformative journey of spiritual growth.

In this chapter, we will explore the biblical wisdom on prioritizing our relationship with God and practically applying it to the challenges of modern life. We'll delve into the importance of focus in achieving spiritual maturity, the art of balancing our mental and physical duties with our heavenly purpose, and proven techniques to help you maintain an unwavering focus on positive, God-honoring changes.

Aligning Our Lives with God's Will

The demands of this world can easily pull us away from the narrow path that leads to life. Like Martha, we can become "worried and upset about many things," neglecting the "one thing needed" - time spent in the presence of our Savior (Luke 10:38-42). Yet, Jesus reminds us that when we "seek first his kingdom and his righteousness, all these things will be given to you as well" (Matthew 6:33).

The key to overcoming the struggle of divided attention is to make God the true center of our lives. This doesn't mean ignoring our earthly responsibilities, but rather, recognizing that when we align our lives with God's purpose, He will grant us the wisdom, strength, and resources to manage our daily duties effectively. By keeping our eyes fixed on the eternal, we can find the balance and clarity needed to navigate the temporal. The temporal of the mind your temportal. Change the mindset and change your life. Now is more important than ever to start focusing on yourself all you have to do is let things play out in your life what is meant to be will be, and once you find inner peace things will truly be what is meant to be. The way you think plays a major role in how your experiencing life. You attract what you feel and you think what you feel. A tip is to start thinking about how you want life to be and it will begin to go that way effortsly. Just by allowing a peaceful mind you allow true guidance. Devine Guidance that you can feel and understanding and know that your life is flowing as it should if something leaves it's not meant to be. Before I begin an author, I had dreams of being a Mindset Coach, I am currently a mindset coach and author, and teacher. The possibilities are endless for you and I.

Practical Disciplines for Spiritual Focus

Maintaining spiritual focus requires intentionality and the cultivation of specific disciplines. Just as a plant needs sunlight, water, and nutrients to thrive, our souls require regular nourishment through spiritual practices. Some of the most powerful tools at our disposal include:

Setting Clear, God-Centered Goals: Habakkuk 2:2 encourages us to "write down the revelation and make it plain." By prayerfully crafting specific, measurable goals that align with God's will, we create a roadmap for spiritual growth.

Establishing a Structured Routine: Proverbs 12:1 reminds us that "whoever loves discipline loves knowledge." A daily rhythm of prayer, Scripture reading, and time in God's presence helps us stay centered and avoid the pitfalls of distraction.

Prioritizing Self-Care: 1 Corinthians 6:19-20 teaches us that our bodies are "temples of the Holy Spirit." By caring for our physical, emotional, and mental well-being, we create the space for the Holy Spirit to work powerfully in our lives.

Practicing Gratitude and Mindfulness: Philippians 4:6-7 encourages us to "present your requests to God with thanksgiving." Cultivating a grateful heart and staying present in the moment keeps our focus on God's goodness, even in difficult circumstances.

Seeking Accountability and Support: Ecclesiastes 4:9-10 reminds us that "two are better than one." Surrounding ourselves with a community of believers who can encourage, challenge, and pray for us is essential for staying the course.

Aligning Every Step with God's Purpose

Ultimately, spiritual growth is not a one-time event, but a lifelong journey of transformation. Each day presents us with countless choices, and it's in the small, seemingly insignificant decisions that we either draw closer to or drift further from God's will. As Paul exhorts in Romans 12:2, we must be "transformed by the renewing of [our] mind," aligning our thoughts, words, and actions with the eternal purpose God has for our lives.

Like the Apostle Paul, who pressed on "toward the goal to win the prize for which God has called [him] heavenward" (Philippians 3:13-14), we must keep our eyes fixed on the heavenly prize, allowing every step we take to be guided by our desire to please and glorify the Lord. When our focus is firmly rooted in God's kingdom and His righteousness, He will make our paths straight and grant us the clarity, strength, and perseverance to fulfill the unique calling He has placed on our hearts.

Chapter 4
The Gift of Forgiveness

Forgiveness is one of the most powerful and transformative gifts we can offer—not only to others, but to ourselves. It has the ability to heal the deepest wounds, clear our hearts of bitterness, and open the doors to growth and happiness. Yet, the practice of forgiveness is often misunderstood or difficult to embrace, especially when we've been hurt deeply. In this chapter, we'll explore the profound role that forgiveness plays in clearing the mind and heart, how holding on to resentment can block our growth, and practical tools for achieving inner peace through the act of forgiving.

The Role of Forgiveness in Clearing the Mind and Heart

Forgiveness is the spiritual practice that frees us from the burden of bitterness and anger. When we forgive, we release ourselves from the chains of past hurts, allowing our hearts to heal. The Scriptures teach us that forgiveness is not just for the person who wronged us, but primarily for our own well-being.

Ephesians 4:31-32 reminds us: "Get rid of all bitterness, rage and anger, brawling and slander, along with every form of malice. Be kind and compassionate to one another, forgiving each other, just as the Divine forgave you."

This passage highlights that bitterness and anger only harm the one holding onto them. The longer we carry these negative emotions, the heavier they become, clouding our hearts and minds. Unforgiveness doesn't hurt the other person as much as it hurts us. It poisons our thoughts, drains our energy, and blocks the flow of peace and joy. When we forgive, we clear the emotional clutter that keeps us from moving forward, creating space for peace, growth, and deeper connection with the Divine.

Imagine a wise sage who, after years of spreading love and compassion in his village, is betrayed by those he trusted. They conspired against him, spreading falsehoods that led to his exile. Instead of harboring resentment, the sage retreats into nature, seeking solace and understanding.

During his time alone, he reflects on the interconnectedness of all beings and the lessons that pain can teach. He realizes that the betrayal, while painful, has given him the opportunity to grow in wisdom and compassion.

Instead of seeking revenge, he greets them with warmth and understanding, saying, "I see now that you acted out of fear and misunderstanding. Let us learn together from this experience."

His choice to forgive not only heals the rift between him and his betrayers but also transforms everyone involved. It's a powerful reminder that forgiveness can lead to collective healing and growth, liberating both the forgiver and the forgiven. Through this act of compassion, he creates a ripple effect of love that brings the community closer together.

His heart was clear, and in doing so, he was able to embrace the fullness of the Divine's purpose for his life.

How Holding on to Resentment Blocks Growth and Happiness

Resentment is a silent killer of personal growth and happiness. It is a weight that we carry, often without realizing how much it drags us down. When we hold on to past hurts, we allow the wounds of the past to shape our present reality. Resentment clouds our thoughts, sours our relationships, and prevents us from fully living the life the Divine has called us to live.

In a serene village nestled between rolling hills, there lived a wise elder known for his deep understanding of the human heart. One day, a troubled young man approached him, burdened by the weight of resentment. He shared his story of being wronged by a close friend, who had taken advantage of his trust.

The elder listened patiently and then told a tale of two villagers. One, named Arin, had amassed a great fortune through hard work, while the other, named Lira, struggled to make ends meet. One fateful day, Lira found herself in desperate need and borrowed a small sum from Arin. Despite her sincere promise to repay, unforeseen circumstances prevented her from doing so.

When Arin learned of Lira's inability to repay the debt, he was furious. Instead of showing compassion, he demanded repayment and threatened to ruin her life. In his anger, he forgot the kindness he had once received from others during his own hardships.

Meanwhile, the village elder observed the situation and decided to intervene. He called Arin to his home and reminded him of a time when he himself had faced dire straits, and how the community had rallied around him. The elder asked him to consider how much lighter his heart would feel if he chose to forgive Lira, rather than burdening himself with anger.

Arin was moved by the elder's words and realized that holding onto resentment only chained him to bitterness. He sought out Lira and, with newfound understanding, forgave her debt. The moment he released his anger, he felt a profound transformation within himself; it was as if a heavy fog had lifted, revealing bright sunlight.

In the days that followed, Arin and Lira began to rebuild their friendship, supporting each other through their struggles. Their bond deepened, and the village thrived as they inspired others to practice forgiveness. The elder watched with a smile, knowing that the true essence of life lay in compassion and understanding.

And so, the lesson echoed throughout the village: to forgive is to free oneself, for only then can the heart truly heal and flourish. The elder often reminded everyone, "When you choose to let go of grudges, you invite peace into your life and illuminate the path for others."

Tools for Achieving Inner Peace Through Forgiveness

Forgiveness is not always easy, especially when the pain runs deep. However, it is a vital step in achieving inner peace. Here are some tools to help you practice forgiveness and clear your heart and mind:

Pray for the Strength to Forgive

Forgiveness often requires a strength we don't possess on our own. The Divine understands this, which is why the Divine offers us the Divine's strength when we are weak. In Luke 17:3-4, the Divine tells us that even if someone sins against us seven times in a day, we must forgive them. It's not about relying on our own ability to forgive but asking the Divine for the strength to do so. Begin by praying, "Divine, I can't forgive on my own, but I trust you to help me. Give me the grace to release this burden."

Write It Down

Sometimes, forgiveness requires a physical act of release. Writing down the pain, the anger, or the resentment you feel toward someone can be a powerful way to process and release it. After writing, you can choose to burn the paper, rip it up, or bury it as a symbolic gesture of letting go. This act of physical release can provide emotional relief and clarity.

Shift Your Perspective

Forgiveness is often difficult because we hold onto the narrative that the other person "deserves" to be punished. But the Divine's grace is greater than our sense of justice. As Isaiah 55:8-9 reminds us, "For my thoughts are not your thoughts, neither are your ways my ways." The Divine's ways are higher than ours. Shift your perspective from a focus on the offense to a focus on the Divine's mercy. Realize that forgiveness frees you from the emotional prison of resentment and allows the Divine's healing to flow into your life.

Choose to Bless, Not Curse

In Romans 12:14, the Apostle Paul instructs us: "Bless those who persecute you; bless and do not curse." One way to practice forgiveness is to intentionally pray for the person who hurt you. Ask the Divine to bless them, to heal their heart, and to guide their steps. This act of blessing will soften your heart and release

the negative hold they have over you. It is difficult to
remain angry at someone you are consistently praying
for.

Remember the Divine's Forgiveness Toward You

In moments of struggle to forgive others, it's essential to reflect on the boundless forgiveness that the Divine extends to us. This profound grace invites us to pause and consider the weight of our own burdens that have been lifted. Think about the times when you have faltered, yet found solace in the understanding that the Divine embraces you without judgment.

As we navigate the complexities of human relationships, let the essence of this divine forgiveness inspire our hearts. When we remember the infinite love and acceptance that the Divine offers, we can find the strength to extend that same grace to others.

If the Divine can release us from our past, present, and future missteps, how can we hold onto grudges against those who have crossed our paths? By embracing this divine perspective, we open ourselves to healing and transformation, allowing forgiveness to flow freely from our hearts and into the world around us.

Forgiveness as Freedom

Forgiveness is a divine gift that brings freedom. It clears the clutter of resentment and bitterness from our hearts, allowing us to experience peace, joy, and spiritual growth. It is not a sign of weakness, but of strength—strength that comes from the Divine. As we forgive, we align ourselves with the Divine's will, experience the Divine's grace, and reflect the Divine's love to the world around us.

Remember that forgiveness is not about forgetting or excusing the wrong, but about releasing the power that the offense holds over your life. It is a choice—a choice that leads to freedom. As you practice forgiveness, know that each step brings you closer to the peace and joy that the Divine desires for you.

Chapter 5
Prioritizing Spiritual Focus in a Distracted World

In today's fast-paced world, filled with distractions at every turn, it is often challenging to maintain spiritual focus. From the pressures of work, family obligations, and social expectations to the pervasive noise of technology, our attention is constantly divided. The demands of daily life can easily overshadow our spiritual aspirations, leading us to feel disconnected from our higher purpose. Yet, it is precisely in this age of distraction that the practice of prioritizing our spiritual well-being becomes more vital than ever. In this chapter, we will explore the ways in which we can stay spiritually grounded amidst life's whirlwind, balancing our worldly responsibilities with the pursuit of spiritual growth.

Aligning Our Lives with Our Spiritual Purpose

The tension between the demands of the material world and our spiritual aspirations is not a new struggle. In the Bible, we find the story of Martha and

Mary (Luke 10:38-42), two sisters who are presented with a choice: one remains focused on serving, while the other chooses to sit at the feet of Jesus. Martha, overwhelmed by the many tasks before her, becomes frustrated with her sister's decision to prioritize spiritual nourishment. Jesus, however, affirms Mary's choice, saying, "Martha, Martha, you are worried and upset about many things, but few things are needed—or indeed only one. Mary has chosen what is better, and it will not be taken away from her" (Luke 10:41-42).

In this passage, we see the importance of spiritual focus in a world full of distractions. The message is not that earthly responsibilities are unimportant, but that they should not come at the cost of our deeper, spiritual needs. Jesus suggests that spiritual nourishment—seeking wisdom, guidance, and presence in the divine—is the "one thing needed." When we center our lives on spiritual growth, it is not a rejection of our duties or relationships, but rather a recognition that everything else flows more smoothly when we remain rooted in our higher purpose.

Jesus also teaches in Matthew 6:33, "But seek first his kingdom and his righteousness, and all these things will be given to you as well." This verse emphasizes the importance of prioritizing spiritual alignment over the pursuit of material wealth, career success, or social approval. The key to overcoming the struggle of divided attention is to align our lives with our spiritual purpose. When we do so, the wisdom, strength, and resources we need to fulfill our earthly duties will be provided to us in abundance.

The Art of Balancing Our Responsibilities with Our Higher Purpose

Balancing the practical demands of life with the pursuit of spiritual growth requires intentionality. It means recognizing that our daily responsibilities—whether it's work, family, or self-care—are not separate from our spiritual path, but rather intertwined with it. The challenge is in maintaining a harmonious relationship between these aspects, ensuring that one does not overwhelm the other.

One of the first steps toward achieving this balance is mindfulness. Mindfulness is the practice of bringing our full attention to the present moment, without judgment or distraction. In a spiritual context, mindfulness allows us to remain aware of our thoughts, actions, and feelings, helping us make decisions that are in alignment with our values and higher purpose. Whether we are working, spending time with family, or engaging in daily tasks, mindfulness helps us to stay connected to our spiritual selves, even in the most mundane moments.

For example, when performing work tasks, instead of rushing through them in a state of stress or distraction, we can approach them with intentionality. We can choose to see our work as an opportunity to express our highest values—whether that's integrity, service, or excellence. By bringing a sense of purpose to each action, we infuse our daily life with spiritual significance.

Another effective practice is time management. In a world filled with endless demands, managing our time wisely becomes a crucial tool for spiritual focus. Setting aside regular moments for prayer, meditation, or reflection helps ensure that we stay spiritually nourished, even as we meet the demands of our professional and personal lives. Prioritizing time for spiritual practices is not about escaping the world, but about ensuring that we are spiritually grounded as we navigate it.

The key to balancing responsibilities with spiritual focus is not perfection, but consistency. Small, daily efforts to reconnect with our higher purpose can yield profound results over time. As we remain steadfast in our spiritual practices, we begin to notice the subtle ways in which our attention shifts. We may find ourselves more present, more compassionate, and more attuned to the deeper meaning behind our daily actions.

Techniques to Maintain Unwavering Spiritual Focus

While life's distractions are inevitable, there are proven techniques to help maintain spiritual focus, even when it feels like everything is pulling us in different directions.

1. **Mindful Breathing**: One of the simplest ways to recenter yourself is through mindful breathing. Taking a few moments throughout the day to focus on your breath can help you stay present and connected to your spiritual center. Even just three deep breaths can calm the mind and restore clarity. This technique can be particularly helpful in moments of stress, helping to break the cycle of overwhelm and bring you back to the present moment.

2. **Daily Reflection**: Setting aside time each day to reflect on your actions, thoughts, and feelings can help you stay aligned with your

spiritual goals. Journaling, prayer, or simply sitting in silence can provide an opportunity for self-examination and spiritual renewal. These moments of reflection are vital for staying on course and for making adjustments when necessary.

3. **Spiritual Community**: Surrounding yourself with a like-minded community can provide support and encouragement along the journey. Whether it's through a religious congregation, a meditation group, or a network of friends who share your spiritual values, having people to share your struggles and successes with can help you stay motivated and focused. Spiritual communities offer a sense of belonging and remind us that we are not alone in our journey.

4. **Acts of Service**: One powerful way to stay spiritually focused is by engaging in acts of service. Helping others not only benefits those around us, but it also nurtures our own spiritual growth. Service reminds us of the interconnectedness of all people and reinforces our commitment to living in

alignment with our higher values.

5. **Gratitude Practice**: Cultivating a daily practice of gratitude is an effective way to maintain spiritual focus. By taking time each day to acknowledge the blessings in our lives, we shift our perspective from what is lacking to what is abundant. Gratitude invites us to see the divine in every moment, no matter how small or ordinary.

Conclusion: The Transformative Power of Spiritual Focus

In the chaos and distractions of modern life, maintaining spiritual focus can seem like an insurmountable task. Yet, it is precisely in these moments of challenge that our spiritual growth is most needed. By aligning our lives with our higher purpose, balancing our worldly duties with our spiritual aspirations, and applying proven techniques to stay focused, we can transform our everyday experiences into opportunities for spiritual growth.

When we make spirituality the center of our lives, we are better equipped to navigate the complexities of the world around us. Through consistent practices of mindfulness, reflection, and service, we create space for our higher wisdom to guide us. As we do so, we find that the path of spiritual growth becomes not just a distant ideal, but a living, breathing reality that informs and transforms every aspect of our lives.

In the end, the journey toward spiritual maturity is not about perfection, but about persistence. It is a journey that asks us to continually realign ourselves with our true purpose and to trust that, as we seek first our higher calling, everything else will fall into place.

Chapter 6
The Role of Positive Thinking

In the grand tapestry of life, the thoughts we entertain are not mere fleeting whims; they are the threads that intricately weave the fabric of our lived experience. Just as the sun rises each day to illuminate the world, our mindset has the power to either light our path with clarity or cast dark shadows that cloud our vision. In this chapter, we explore the transformative power of positive thinking—how it shapes our reality, enhances our lives, and guides us toward greater peace, fulfillment, and purpose.

1. How Thoughts Shape Reality

Every thought we entertain is like a seed planted in the fertile soil of our consciousness. These seeds, whether they are sown consciously or unconsciously, grow and manifest as experiences that shape the contours of our reality. If we nurture these thoughts with intention, positivity, and care, they will bloom into a rich and vibrant reality that mirrors the beauty of our inner world. However, when our thoughts are rooted in negativity or doubt, they can grow into experiences that hinder our progress and cloud our sense of possibility.

The universe, in all its mystery, responds to the energy we project through our thoughts, beliefs, and emotions. This is the profound interplay of creation. Our thoughts act as the brushstrokes of our life's masterpiece, with each thought contributing to the greater picture. When we choose to focus on positive thoughts, we begin to attract experiences that reflect that positivity—transforming challenges into opportunities, struggles into growth, and sorrow into moments of deep insight and joy.

This sacred dance of creation—where our thoughts and emotions shape the material world—reminds us of our incredible power to influence not only our inner experiences but also the outer circumstances of our lives. The ability to consciously direct our thoughts is the key to manifesting a reality that aligns with our higher aspirations and deepest values.

2. Insights into How Thoughts Shape Our Reality

The Law of Attraction: Like Attracts Like

One of the most widely discussed principles in the realm of positive thinking is the Law of Attraction. This concept suggests that the energy we emit through our thoughts and emotions attracts similar energies from the universe. In other words, like attracts like. When we radiate positive, uplifting thoughts, we invite positivity into our lives—whether in the form of opportunities, relationships, or experiences that nurture and support our growth. Conversely, when our thoughts are filled with negativity, fear, or doubt, we often find ourselves encountering situations that reflect those very same energies.

The Law of Attraction is not about wishful thinking or mere positive affirmations; it is a deeply rooted principle that operates within the universal laws of energy and vibration. When we consciously align our thoughts with our desires and dreams, we create a magnetic pull that draws those desires toward us. It is through cultivating a mindset of abundance, gratitude, and possibility that we unlock the door to a reality that mirrors our highest vision.

Mindfulness and Presence: Observing and Shaping Our Thoughts

To shape our reality through positive thinking, we must first cultivate a heightened awareness of our thoughts. Mindfulness, the practice of being fully present in the moment, allows us to step back and observe our thoughts without judgment or attachment. In doing so, we create the space necessary to break free from negative or unhelpful patterns of thinking and replace them with more constructive, empowering beliefs.

When we become mindful of our thoughts, we realize that we are not our thoughts—they are simply transient patterns that arise and pass away. This awareness gives us the power to choose the thoughts we want to entertain, much like a gardener selecting the seeds to plant in a garden. Through mindful observation, we can begin to shift our mindset, transforming negative thoughts into more positive ones and, by extension, shifting the course of our lives.

Mindfulness also helps us develop greater compassion and patience with ourselves, allowing us to see our imperfections as opportunities for growth rather than as sources of frustration. By being present with our thoughts, we can bring conscious awareness to the ways in which we sabotage ourselves, and through that awareness, we can change the trajectory of our experiences.

Reframing Challenges: Turning Obstacles Into Opportunities

One of the most powerful ways to harness the transformative power of positive thinking is through the practice of reframing. Reframing involves shifting our perspective on a situation, seeing it not as an obstacle but as an opportunity for growth. Instead of focusing on the difficulty or the pain, reframing encourages us to look for the lessons and the hidden blessings in every experience.

When faced with challenges, we can ask ourselves empowering questions like: What can I learn from this? How is this situation serving my highest good? What opportunities for growth are embedded in this challenge? By changing our focus, we shift our emotional response to the situation, which, in turn, influences how we experience it. A positive mindset allows us to see beyond the surface, uncovering the deeper meaning behind difficult circumstances and transforming them into stepping stones toward our greater purpose.

The Power of Gratitude

Gratitude is one of the most potent tools in the arsenal of positive thinking. When we focus on what we are grateful for, we shift our attention away from lack and scarcity toward abundance and fulfillment. Gratitude opens our hearts to the beauty and blessings already present in our lives, amplifying the positive energy we emit and attracting more of the same.

The simple practice of daily gratitude—whether through journaling, prayer, or silent reflection—can radically shift our perspective. By acknowledging the good in our lives, no matter how small, we begin to see the world through a lens of abundance rather than deficiency. This shift in mindset not only brings greater peace and joy but also serves as a magnet for more positive experiences to flow into our lives.

3. Integrating Positive Thinking into Daily Life

Positive thinking is not a one-time effort; it is a way of being. To integrate it into our daily lives, we must cultivate habits that reinforce a positive mindset, even in the face of adversity. Here are some practical ways to embody positive thinking:

Start the Day with Intention: Set a positive tone for your day by affirming your goals, your gratitude, and your commitment to living with purpose. Visualize yourself navigating the day with confidence, peace, and clarity.

Surround Yourself with Positivity: The people and environments we engage with have a profound impact on our mindset. Surround yourself with individuals who uplift and inspire you, and create spaces that nourish your soul.

Practice Self-Compassion: Treat yourself with the same kindness and understanding that you would offer to a dear friend. Positive thinking is not about perfection, but about embracing the journey with love and patience.

Reframe Negative Thoughts: When negative thoughts arise, practice reframing them. Ask yourself, What is the lesson here? How can I grow from this situation? Shifting your perspective can transform challenges into valuable opportunities.

Cultivate Mindfulness: Be present with your thoughts, emotions, and experiences. Mindfulness allows you to become aware of negative patterns and replace them with more constructive, empowering ones.

The role of positive thinking in shaping our reality is both profound and powerful. By consciously directing our thoughts, we tap into the limitless potential that lies within us, transforming our lives from ordinary to extraordinary. The universe responds to the energy we emit—positive thoughts lead to positive experiences, while negative thoughts attract challenges and limitations. Through mindfulness, gratitude, and reframing, we can shift our mindset, overcoming obstacles and creating a reality that reflects our highest aspirations. The choice is ours: we can continue to be shaped by external circumstances, or we can consciously create the life we desire by cultivating a mindset rooted in positivity and possibility. The journey begins with a single thought—and each thought we nurture has the power to transform our world.

Chapter 7
Accountability and Self-Awareness

In the intricate journey of the soul, accountability serves as a beacon—a light that illuminates the path toward personal growth, transformation, and deeper self-understanding. It is an invitation to pause, reflect, and embrace the lessons that are woven into the fabric of our past actions and decisions. It invites us to step into our own power, not as perfect beings, but as conscious creators of our own lives.

Accepting Responsibility for Past Actions and Mistakes

The journey towards true accountability begins with the simple yet profound act of accepting responsibility. This is not an act of self-criticism or condemnation, but rather a loving embrace of all that we have been, done, and chosen. In this acceptance, we come to understand that every action—every decision, every misstep—holds a lesson that can deepen our understanding of ourselves and the world around us.

Accepting responsibility for our past does not mean dwelling in guilt or shame. These emotions, while natural responses to our mistakes, can also become heavy burdens that keep us anchored in the past. Instead, accountability allows us to release these burdens. When we let go of the need to punish ourselves, we create space for healing and growth. Acknowledging our missteps is not an act of self-judgment but one of self-compassion. By embracing our flaws with kindness, we transform them from sources of pain into opportunities for evolution.

Each misstep we have made becomes a stepping stone in our journey—an essential part of the tapestry of our lives. When we accept this truth, we move from the place of victimhood to empowerment. We recognize that our mistakes do not define us, but rather, they refine us, helping us to become more aware, more compassionate, and more attuned to the deeper wisdom within.

As we step into accountability, we begin to see patterns—repeated choices or behaviors that have shaped the course of our lives. This awareness is the first key to transformation. It becomes the compass that guides us forward, helping us to make more conscious decisions that align with the person we are becoming, not the person we once were.

How Accountability Empowers Personal Growth

When we hold ourselves accountable, we take ownership of our lives. We acknowledge that we are the architects of our journey and that, while we cannot control every circumstance, we always have the power to choose how we respond. Accountability empowers us because it places the reins of our life squarely in our own hands. No longer do we remain passive observers of our own story—we become active participants, creating the life we desire from a place of conscious intention.

This sense of ownership fosters resilience. Life, inevitably, will present challenges, setbacks, and moments of doubt. However, when we hold ourselves accountable, we see these challenges not as insurmountable obstacles, but as opportunities for transformation. We understand that setbacks are not signs of failure but of growth in progress. Each difficulty we face is an invitation to dig deeper, to reflect, and to rise stronger.

Moreover, in the spiritual realm, accountability is deeply intertwined with the concept of interconnectedness. It is the understanding that every action we take, every word we speak, ripples out into the world around us, affecting not just ourselves, but those we encounter. Accountability, then, is not just a personal practice; it is a collective one. Our choices have an impact far beyond our own lives, and in embracing accountability, we strive to make choices that are intentional and aligned with our highest values.

The Role of Self-Awareness in Accountability

Self-awareness is the bedrock upon which true accountability is built. To hold ourselves accountable, we must first develop a keen awareness of our thoughts, emotions, and actions. This awareness is not about judging ourselves for our imperfections, but about cultivating an honest, compassionate understanding of who we are. By observing our behaviors without judgment, we begin to see the patterns that shape our reality and recognize where we may need to make adjustments in order to live more consciously.

Through self-awareness, we also gain insight into our motivations, desires, and fears. Why do we make the choices we do? What are the underlying beliefs that drive our actions? By asking these questions, we begin to uncover the deeper layers of our psyche and understand the forces that shape our lives. This knowledge becomes the foundation for change, allowing us to make intentional, empowered choices that reflect the person we wish to become.

Self-awareness, when practiced with patience and love, brings us closer to the truth of who we are. It allows us to separate our true essence from the stories we tell ourselves or the roles we play in the world. We begin to understand that we are not defined by our past mistakes, nor by the labels others place on us. We are, instead, dynamic beings, always in the process of becoming, and through self-awareness, we come to know ourselves as we truly are—whole, worthy, and always capable of growth.

Accountability as a Spiritual Practice

In the grander spiritual context, accountability is not merely a moral or ethical practice, but a sacred one. It is an acknowledgment that we are participants in a larger cosmic order, where our actions matter and have far-reaching consequences. Our lives are interconnected with the lives of others, and our choices contribute to the collective story of humanity.

When we approach accountability with this understanding, it becomes a practice of integrity— acting in alignment with our highest truth, even when it is difficult. It means showing up fully, embracing our humanity, and owning the choices we make, knowing that we are part of something much greater than ourselves. As we do this, we learn to act with more compassion, more mindfulness, and more intention. We become more attuned to the impact of our actions on others, recognizing that our own personal growth is inseparable from the well-being of the world around us.

In embracing accountability, we also deepen our relationship with ourselves and with the divine. We move beyond the limitations of ego and fear, stepping into a space of authenticity and trust. We trust that, even in our imperfections, we are exactly where we need to be, and that every step of our journey, every decision, every mistake, is a sacred part of our soul's evolution.

Conclusion

Accountability is the key to unlocking our personal power. It is the acknowledgment that we are the creators of our own lives, and that our choices, both past and present, shape the reality we experience. Through accountability, we cultivate self-awareness, transform our mistakes into opportunities for growth, and become more intentional in our actions. It is a spiritual practice that connects us to the greater web of existence, inviting us to live with integrity, purpose, and compassion.

When we embrace accountability, we step into the fullness of who we are meant to be—whole, empowered, and deeply connected to the truth that we are always capable of growth and transformation.

52

Chapter 8
The Mindset Reset Process

In the journey of personal growth, the first step toward transformation is recognizing the need for change. We often find ourselves stuck in cycles of negativity, self-doubt, or limiting beliefs, unaware that we possess the power to initiate a profound shift. Yet, it is precisely in those moments of awareness—the realization that something within us needs to change—that the process of personal transformation begins. This chapter will guide you through six essential steps to reset your mindset, helping you break free from old patterns and embrace a more positive, empowering, and fulfilling life.

Step 1: Acknowledgment

The journey to resetting your mindset begins with acknowledgment. This first step is about creating a space of awareness and honesty. Pause for a moment and reflect on the thoughts, beliefs, and attitudes that currently shape your life. Are there recurring negative patterns that hold you back? Do you often catch yourself feeling unworthy, inadequate, or fearful?

Identifying these patterns is crucial to understanding their impact on your life.

Take a few minutes to write down these negative thoughts and feelings. Seeing them on paper can sometimes make them feel less overpowering. It also allows you to reflect on how these thoughts have shaped your choices, relationships, and overall sense of well-being. Acknowledging the presence of these limiting beliefs is not about self-criticism or judgment; it is about understanding their role in your life and realizing that they no longer serve you. This is the first step toward liberation.

Acknowledgment is not just about recognizing negative patterns; it is also about honoring the positive aspects of yourself. Take time to reflect on the strengths, talents, and achievements you've cultivated throughout your life. Even the smallest victories—moments when you've shown resilience, compassion, or courage—are worth recognizing. By acknowledging both your strengths and areas for growth, you develop a more complete and authentic sense of self. This balance of self-awareness fosters self-acceptance, which is essential for any true mindset reset.

This step requires a profound level of self-compassion. Instead of harshly judging yourself for past mistakes or current shortcomings, you learn to treat yourself with the kindness and understanding you would offer to a dear friend. Embrace your imperfections and acknowledge that they are part of your unique journey. In this space of non-judgment, you allow yourself the freedom to grow.

Step 2: Reframing

Once you've acknowledged your current mindset, the next step is reframing your perspective. Reframing is the practice of shifting your focus from a negative or limiting belief to a more positive, empowering one. It involves consciously choosing to view a situation from a different angle—one that fosters growth, possibility, and optimism.

For example, if you find yourself thinking, *"I'll never be good enough,"* try reframing this to something like, *"I am constantly growing and learning, and I am enough exactly as I am right now."* This simple shift in language can have a profound impact on how you feel and act. Reframing helps you break free from the habitual patterns of negative thinking that hold you back and replace them with thoughts that inspire positive action and self-belief.

This step requires mindfulness and patience. It's not about instantly erasing negative thoughts but rather recognizing them when they arise and choosing to consciously redirect your attention. With practice, reframing becomes a natural response to negativity. Over time, you'll train your brain to focus on the possibilities rather than the limitations, cultivating a mindset that is more resilient, positive, and capable of overcoming challenges.

Step 3: Setting Intentions

The next step is setting clear and purposeful intentions. It is one thing to acknowledge that a shift is needed, and another thing entirely to take deliberate action. Setting intentions means deciding, with clarity and purpose, what you want to manifest in your life. Unlike vague goals, intentions are grounded in a deep sense of alignment with your true values and desires. They are the compass that guides you through the challenges and distractions of daily life.

When setting intentions, be specific and aligned with your personal truth. For example, instead of saying, *"I want to be more successful,"* try something like, *"I intend to work with focus and passion on projects that bring me joy and contribute meaningfully to my community."* This intention is rooted in purpose, and it reflects your true values. It gives you something tangible to work toward and anchors you when doubt or fear arises.

Intentions act as a magnet, drawing you closer to your goals and helping you to stay on track even when obstacles appear. By setting them with mindfulness and clarity, you are aligning your mindset with your deepest aspirations.

Step 4: Releasing Resistance

Often, the biggest barrier to a mindset reset is resistance. This resistance can take many forms—fear of failure, fear of the unknown, or even the discomfort of change. But the truth is, resistance is a natural part of the growth process. It arises because our minds are wired to seek familiarity and safety, even if those familiar patterns no longer serve us.

Releasing resistance involves acknowledging the fear or discomfort that arises when you step outside of your comfort zone. Instead of avoiding or fighting it, you learn to sit with it, allowing it to pass without letting it dictate your actions. This process is about developing a relationship with discomfort, understanding that growth often requires us to push through it.

To release resistance, practice deep breathing, mindfulness, or any other technique that helps you stay grounded in the present moment. With each step you take outside of your comfort zone, you build resilience and cultivate the courage needed to move forward.

Step 5: Embracing Gratitude

Gratitude is one of the most powerful tools in resetting your mindset. It shifts your focus from what you lack to what you already have, cultivating a sense of abundance and appreciation. Gratitude helps you to see the beauty in everyday moments and reminds you that you are supported by a universe that is always working in your favor.

Start each day by writing down three things you are grateful for. They can be big or small—anything that brings you joy, peace, or contentment. By making gratitude a daily practice, you train your mind to seek out the positive, to notice the good in yourself and the world around you. Over time, this practice will help to shift your overall perspective, moving you from scarcity to abundance, from fear to trust.

Step 6: Taking Inspired Action

The final step in the mindset reset process is taking inspired action. This means moving forward with purpose and clarity, aligned with the intentions you've set and the mindset you've cultivated. Inspired action is not about forcing results or striving in a state of constant hustle; it's about trusting that when you take steps toward your goals with intention, the universe will support you in ways you may not fully understand yet.

Inspired action comes from a place of trust and confidence. It is guided by the belief that you are on the right path, and that each step, no matter how small, brings you closer to your vision. By taking consistent, inspired action, you begin to create the life you desire—one thought, one intention, and one step at a time.

Conclusion

Resetting your mindset is a journey that requires patience, practice, and commitment. It is about creating a new relationship with your thoughts, your beliefs, and your actions. By acknowledging where you are, reframing your perspective, setting clear intentions, releasing resistance, embracing gratitude, and taking inspired action, you open yourself up to the incredible possibilities that lie ahead. Your mindset is not a fixed trait—it is a powerful tool that you can shape and refine as you grow. By taking these six steps, you begin to shift the very fabric of your reality, creating a life that is aligned with your true purpose and filled with the richness of possibility.

Chapter 9
Taking Action for Lasting Change

When it comes to transforming our mindset, action is the bridge between intention and reality. While cultivating a positive mindset through affirmations, visualization, and reflection is essential, it is through consistent, deliberate action that we truly bring our aspirations to life. Action is not just a practical step in the process; it is the manifestation of our inner work. It is what propels us forward, solidifies our commitment to change, and brings momentum to our personal growth.

Why Is Action Essential to Mindset Transformation?

Taking action is crucial for mindset transformation because it shifts us from passive thinking to active doing. It's one thing to affirm that we are capable, confident, or worthy; it's another to take tangible steps that align with those beliefs. Action turns our thoughts into results. It demonstrates to ourselves and the universe that we are serious about creating change and ready to face challenges head-on.

Action also helps us overcome the inertia that often accompanies change. It's easy to get stuck in the planning phase, dreaming of what could be, without ever moving toward what we desire. This inaction can feel paralyzing, leaving us in a perpetual state of "someday." But when we take deliberate steps, even small ones, we begin to break free from the grip of doubt and fear. Each action reinforces our belief in our abilities and builds our confidence, making it easier to continue on the path toward transformation.

Ultimately, action fosters a sense of empowerment. It helps us take ownership of our journey, rather than waiting for external circumstances to shift. When we act, we are declaring our intentions to the world and ourselves. With each step we take, we build resilience and determination, reinforcing our commitment to personal growth.

Examples of Small, Daily Actions That Can Lead to Meaningful Change

Transformation doesn't happen overnight, and lasting change doesn't require drastic leaps. Often, the most meaningful shifts occur when we incorporate small, consistent actions into our daily routines. These seemingly small steps compound over time, creating a ripple effect that leads to profound growth.

Mindfulness Practice: Setting aside just five to ten minutes each morning for mindfulness or meditation can help center your mind, calm your thoughts, and align you with your deeper intentions for the day.

Journaling: Writing down your thoughts, feelings, or experiences can provide clarity, helping you gain insights into your mindset and emotional state. Journaling can also be a powerful tool for self-reflection and personal accountability.

Daily Movement: Whether it's a brisk walk, yoga, or a short workout, moving your body every day helps clear mental fog, boost your energy, and enhance your mood. It's a physical reminder that you are capable and active in your own transformation.

Reading for Growth: Dedicate a few minutes each day to reading books or articles that inspire and educate you. Whether it's a self-help book, spiritual teachings, or something related to your professional goals, daily reading can stimulate your mind and expand your understanding.

Gratitude Practice: Start each day by acknowledging three things you are grateful for. Practicing gratitude shifts your focus from what's lacking to what's abundant, creating a positive foundation for the day.

Connecting with Others: Make a habit of reaching out to a friend, family member, or mentor for connection, support, or encouragement. Building a network of people who lift you up can provide the motivation and accountability needed to stay on course.

These daily actions, while small, are powerful because they reinforce the mindset shift you are working to create. The key is consistency. Over time, these actions become habits that support your overall transformation and help you align with the person you are becoming.

Acting as If You're Already Living Your Desired Life

One of the most powerful strategies for creating lasting change is to act as if you're already living your desired life. This approach encourages you to embody the qualities, behaviors, and attitudes of the person you want to become, even before those qualities are fully manifested in your external reality.

Imagine that the goals you've set for yourself—whether they are related to health, career, relationships, or personal development—are already a part of your life. How would you show up each day if you were already living the life you desire? What would your thoughts, actions, and behaviors look like? How would you speak, dress, and carry yourself?

By acting "as if," you begin to step into the energy of your future self, and that energy has a magnetic pull. When you act as though you are already aligned with your goals, you begin to attract the people, opportunities, and circumstances that support your vision. More importantly, you cultivate the inner confidence and mindset that make success inevitable.

This doesn't mean pretending or faking it in a superficial way. Rather, it's about tapping into the essence of who you want to become, and then letting that energy guide your actions. Acting as if aligns your thoughts, emotions, and behaviors with your highest potential, and in doing so, you bring that potential to life.

Conclusion: The Power of Taking Action

Ultimately, the process of resetting your mindset requires both internal and external shifts. Positive thinking, self-reflection, and intention-setting are essential, but without action, they remain abstract concepts. It is through action that we ground our desires in reality and make them tangible. By taking consistent, purposeful steps toward our goals, no matter how small, we build the momentum needed for lasting change.

Remember, transformation is not a destination but a journey—one that unfolds with every choice and action you take. When you embrace the power of action, you are no longer waiting for life to change; you are actively creating it. With each small step, you move closer to the person you are meant to be, and your life begins to reflect the transformation you've always dreamed of.

Chapter 10
Handling Life's Challenges

Life is an unpredictable journey, filled with moments of joy, challenge, and everything in between. Stress, setbacks, and emotional triggers are an inevitable part of the human experience. How we navigate these obstacles plays a critical role in shaping our personal growth, resilience, and overall well-being. This chapter explores how to handle life's challenges by gaining a deeper understanding of stress and emotional triggers, and learning how to respond with greater awareness and control.

Learning to Navigate Stress, Setbacks, and Emotional Triggers

Stress is a natural part of life. Whether it's work-related pressures, personal relationship struggles, or the unexpected curveballs life throws our way, stress is something we all encounter. But it's not just the presence of stress that impacts us—it's how we respond to it. When we are stressed or faced with setbacks, we often feel overwhelmed, helpless, or even defeated. However, stress doesn't have to be our enemy. In fact, how we manage stress, setbacks, and emotional triggers can become a source of strength and transformation.

The first step in navigating stress is understanding its nature. Stress often arises from situations where we feel a lack of control, whether it's a demanding project at work, a conflict with a loved one, or an unexpected life change. Emotional triggers, such as past trauma or unresolved feelings, can also amplify our stress, making it harder to think clearly and respond calmly. However, recognizing that stress is a natural response to these situations—and that we have the ability to choose how we react—is a powerful realization.

Once we understand stress, the next step is to acknowledge that setbacks are part of the process, not the end of the journey. In every challenge lies an opportunity for growth. When we reframe setbacks as stepping stones, we start to see them not as obstacles but as lessons that build our resilience. In moments of stress or disappointment, it's essential to remember that we are not defined by our struggles. How we choose to respond in the face of adversity determines our growth.

One of the most powerful ways to navigate stress and emotional triggers is through spiritual practices. These practices offer us the tools to detach from the immediacy of emotional reactions and gain a broader perspective on our challenges. Spirituality provides a sense of inner peace and grounding, helping us to see beyond the moment of stress and find solace in the knowledge that challenges are temporary, and growth is possible.

Key Strategies for Handling Stress and Emotional Triggers

1. Identifying Triggers

The first step in managing stress and emotional triggers is awareness. Keeping a journal to track emotional responses can be an invaluable tool. By noting the situations, people, or events that trigger stress or negative emotions, you begin to identify patterns that can help you better understand your reactions. Awareness is the foundation of change. Once we know our triggers, we can begin to take proactive steps to manage our responses rather than letting them control us.

2. Mindfulness Practices

Mindfulness techniques, such as meditation, deep-breathing exercises, or simply pausing to focus on the present moment, can significantly reduce anxiety and stress. These practices teach us to become observers of our thoughts and emotions rather than being consumed by them. In the midst of chaos, mindfulness allows us to step back and gain clarity. When we cultivate a regular mindfulness practice, we train ourselves to be more present and grounded, reducing the mental noise that can cloud our judgment during stressful times.

For example, when feeling stressed at work or overwhelmed by an argument with a loved one, taking a few moments to close your eyes and breathe deeply can help slow the mind and bring a sense of calm. This simple act of pausing provides an opportunity to re-center and approach the situation with more clarity and composure.

3. Seeking Support

It's essential to remember that we are not meant to navigate life's challenges alone. Building a support network of friends, family, or professionals can provide emotional safety and perspective when times get tough. Sometimes, just talking to someone who listens without judgment can be incredibly healing. A strong support system can offer encouragement, solutions, or simply the comfort of knowing you're not alone in your struggles.

Whether it's seeking advice, venting, or just being heard, connecting with others can help release the tension we hold inside. It can also remind us that we're all navigating this journey together, and it's okay to lean on others for support when we need it.

Tools for Remaining Centered and Maintaining a Peaceful Mindset

1. Meditation and Prayer

Meditation and prayer are two powerful spiritual tools that help calm the mind and center the soul. These practices allow us to step outside of our daily worries and reconnect with our higher selves. Meditation, in particular, helps to quiet the mind, reducing the mental clutter that often accompanies stress. Prayer, on the other hand, invites a sense of surrender and trust in something greater than ourselves, providing a sense of peace and reassurance.

Both practices help foster resilience, offering strength during times of difficulty and providing clarity when we feel lost or confused. By incorporating meditation or prayer into our daily routine, we build an internal sanctuary that we can turn to in times of stress.

2. Gratitude Practice

Gratitude is a transformative practice that shifts our focus from what's wrong to what's right in our lives. In moments of stress, practicing gratitude helps to reframe our perspective and brings us back to what truly matters. Keeping a gratitude journal, where you write down three things you are thankful for each day, can be a simple yet powerful tool for maintaining a peaceful mindset. This practice helps to reduce the emotional weight of challenges by highlighting the positive aspects of life, no matter how small.

3. Compassionate Self-Talk

Finally, learning to speak to ourselves with kindness and compassion is essential for emotional well-being. When we face challenges, it's easy to fall into negative self-talk or self-blame. However, practicing self-compassion helps us respond to setbacks with gentleness. Instead of criticizing ourselves for not "doing better" or "being stronger," we can recognize that we are human, and it's okay to stumble. Treating ourselves with the same compassion we would offer to a friend helps to cultivate resilience and emotional balance.

Conclusion

Life's challenges are inevitable, but our responses to them are not. By embracing practices that promote mindfulness, gratitude, and compassion, we can navigate stress, setbacks, and emotional triggers with greater ease and resilience. Spirituality, in all its forms, provides us with the tools to transform difficulties into opportunities for growth. Through reflection, self-awareness, and conscious action, we become more adept at handling life's inevitable ups and downs, emerging stronger, wiser, and more peaceful with each challenge we overcome.

Chapter 11
Cultivating Inner Peace

In a world filled with noise, chaos, and constant demands, the pursuit of inner peace has become more than just a luxury—it's a necessity. Achieving inner peace is not an overnight process, but rather a transformative journey that offers profound benefits to every aspect of our lives. When we cultivate peace within ourselves, we unlock the ability to navigate life's challenges with greater clarity, resilience, and grace. This inner peace becomes a powerful force that not only enhances our well-being but also enriches our relationships and deepens our connection to the world around us.

The Benefits of Achieving Inner Peace and Its Impact on Your Life and Relationships

The benefits of achieving inner peace are manifold, influencing not only your mental and emotional state but also the way you interact with others. When you are at peace, your internal world reflects a calmness that makes you less reactive to external stressors. Life's challenges may still arise, but instead of becoming overwhelmed by them, you can approach them with clarity and composure. This mental calmness allows you to make thoughtful decisions, reduce anxiety, and maintain a sense of control over your life.

Inner peace also fosters emotional resilience. When you are in a state of peace, you are less likely to be shaken by setbacks or difficulties. Instead of succumbing to frustration, anger, or defensiveness in the face of conflict, you are more able to respond with empathy, understanding, and a sense of perspective. This shift in how you respond to challenges can strengthen your relationships, both personal and professional.

When you cultivate peace within yourself, you radiate that peace outwardly, attracting harmony and positivity in your interactions. As you become more centered and self-assured, you find that you have the capacity to handle conflicts and misunderstandings with patience and compassion. This emotional steadiness fosters healthier, more fulfilling relationships, creating an environment where love, trust, and respect can thrive.

In essence, inner peace serves as the foundation for a more peaceful, loving, and fulfilling life. It creates a ripple effect, enriching not only your own life but the lives of those around you.

Meditation, Mindfulness, and Other Peace-Promoting Practices

Cultivating inner peace requires intention and practice. Meditation and mindfulness are two of the most powerful tools we have to quiet the mind and reconnect with our true essence. These practices, when integrated into daily life, can significantly enhance our sense of peace and tranquility.

Meditation: A Pathway to Stillness and Clarity

Meditation is a practice that encourages stillness, focus, and deep relaxation. It involves turning inward, quieting the mind, and observing thoughts without attachment or judgment. By cultivating this sense of presence, you allow yourself to detach from the noise and distractions of daily life, entering a state of deep peace.

There are many different forms of meditation, each offering its own benefits. Guided meditation, for example, uses the voice of a teacher or guide to lead you through a series of visualizations or affirmations. This can be particularly helpful for beginners, as it offers a structured approach. Transcendental meditation involves the repetition of a mantra, helping to clear the mind and elevate consciousness. Loving-kindness meditation focuses on developing compassion for yourself and others, which can have a profound impact on your relationships and emotional well-being.

Meditation, in whatever form it takes, allows you to find stillness in the midst of life's chaos. It helps to calm the nervous system, reduce stress, and create space for clarity and insight. Regular meditation practice can transform your ability to handle challenges with grace and resilience, fostering a deeper sense of inner peace.

Mindfulness: Being Fully Present in the Moment

Mindfulness is the practice of being fully present and engaged in whatever you are doing, without judgment or distraction. It's about slowing down and paying attention to the present moment with openness and acceptance. Mindfulness can be practiced in virtually any situation, whether you are eating, walking, working, or even doing household chores.

The beauty of mindfulness is that it allows you to break free from autopilot mode—the tendency to go through the motions without truly experiencing life. When you are mindful, you bring a sense of awareness to everything you do, which helps you appreciate life's simple pleasures and moments of beauty. Whether you're savoring a cup of coffee or feeling the warmth of the sun on your skin, mindfulness teaches you to embrace life with presence and gratitude.

In moments of stress, mindfulness can help you pause, take a breath, and re-center yourself before reacting impulsively. By observing your thoughts and feelings without judgment, you create space for peace and calm, even in the midst of chaos.

Other Practices That Promote Inner Peace

In addition to meditation and mindfulness, there are several other practices that can support your journey toward inner peace:

Breathing Exercises: Deep, intentional breathing can activate the parasympathetic nervous system, which promotes relaxation and reduces stress. Simple breathing techniques, like inhaling for a count of four, holding for four, and exhaling for four, can quickly calm your mind and body. **Gratitude Practice**: Focusing on what you're grateful for shifts your attention away from what's lacking in your life and brings you into alignment with abundance. By taking time each day to acknowledge the blessings you have—no matter how small—you cultivate a mindset of peace and contentment. **Spiritual Practices**: Prayer, affirmations, and connecting with your spiritual community can all foster a sense of peace. These practices help you reconnect with your sense of purpose and strengthen your trust in the greater flow of life. **Self-Care**: Taking time for yourself—whether through exercise, rest, hobbies, or creative expression—allows you to recharge and cultivate inner peace. Self-care isn't a luxury; it's a necessity for maintaining your emotional and mental well-being.

Nature and Quiet Time: Spending time in nature or simply sitting in silence can be incredibly grounding. Nature's inherent peace helps to recalibrate our inner state, reminding us of life's simplicity and interconnectedness.

Embracing the Journey of Inner Peace

Achieving inner peace is not a destination but a journey—one that requires ongoing practice, patience, and self-compassion. It's a path that invites you to slow down, become more aware of your inner landscape, and choose peace in every moment.

When you prioritize your inner peace, you not only create a life filled with greater joy, clarity, and resilience, but you also become a source of peace for others. The energy you cultivate within yourself can inspire and uplift those around you, creating a ripple effect that fosters harmony and love in the world.

In the end, cultivating inner peace is not about escaping life's challenges but about facing them with a calm, centered heart. It is about embracing the ebb and flow of life with grace and compassion, knowing that no matter what comes your way, you have the power to remain grounded and peaceful.

Chapter 12
Living and Thriving with a Reset Mindset

In this pivotal chapter, we explore the transformative power of adopting a reset mindset, illustrated through heartfelt narratives and uplifting lessons that resonate deeply within us. A reset mindset is not merely a change of perspective—it is the key to unlocking the potential that lies dormant within each of us. It is the courage to begin anew, to rise after a fall, and to see every challenge as an opportunity for growth. Through the stories of real people who have faced life's toughest trials, we will see that transformation is not just possible but inevitable for those who commit to shifting their mindset.

Real Life Stories of Transformation and Success Through Mindset Resetting

Sometimes, it takes the darkest moments to reveal our brightest strengths. Many people have faced deep personal struggles—loss, failure, illness, or adversity—but through the act of resetting their mindset, they found their way to not only survive but thrive. These stories are not just about overcoming obstacles; they are about the courage to reinvent oneself and the tenacity to rebuild from within.

One such story is that of Emily, a woman who lost her job in the wake of a corporate downsizing. Initially devastated, she spent weeks in self-doubt, wondering what her future held. But instead of succumbing to the feelings of inadequacy that often accompany such loss, Emily made the brave decision to view this setback as an opportunity for change. She enrolled in a course to learn a new skill set, reconnected with old passions, and ultimately pivoted into a career that gave her more joy and fulfillment than she had ever experienced in her previous job. Emily's journey was not without its struggles, but the reset in her mindset helped her see that her worth was not tied to one role or circumstance. By embracing her own ability to adapt and grow, Emily found success in a way she had never imagined.

Then there's Jake, who struggled with an addiction for years, feeling trapped in a cycle of self-sabotage. His turning point came when he realized that his mindset was keeping him stuck—he needed to stop seeing himself as a victim of his circumstances. With the support of a local recovery group, Jake began to shift his mindset from one of self-loathing to one of self-compassion and resilience. He took daily steps toward recovery, not only abstaining from his addiction but also rebuilding his relationships and rebuilding trust in himself. Today, Jake is not only sober but also mentoring others who face similar battles, showing them that it's never too late to reset and reclaim your life.

These stories highlight an essential truth: transformation is possible when we choose to reset our mindset. It is through this mindset shift that we unlock the strength to overcome, adapt, and thrive—no matter the circumstances.

Building a Community of Support and Connection

No journey of transformation is meant to be walked alone. The reset mindset thrives within a community of support—people who uplift, encourage, and inspire each other. This section emphasizes the vital importance of cultivating such networks, where connection is rooted in empathy, understanding, and shared experiences.

Meet Sarah, who, after a painful divorce, felt isolated and disconnected from the world around her. It wasn't until she joined a women's support group that her healing truly began. In this community, Sarah found a space where her vulnerability was met with compassion, not judgment. Through the shared stories and collective wisdom of the group, Sarah began to realize that her struggles were not a reflection of her worth but part of a much larger, universal human experience. The group became a sanctuary where she not only healed but also rediscovered her strength. Today, Sarah is an advocate for others going through similar experiences, creating her own support network where people can find connection and healing.

Supportive communities like these are not just places of comfort—they are crucibles for growth. They offer the safety and encouragement needed to take risks, explore new possibilities, and tackle challenges that may have seemed insurmountable alone. In these environments, vulnerability is seen as a strength, and success is celebrated as a collective achievement. It is through the bonds we create with others that we truly begin to flourish.

The Journey Continues: Embracing Lifelong Growth and Continuous Improvement

A reset mindset is not a destination; it is a lifelong journey. Personal growth is dynamic, and the commitment to continuous improvement allows us to keep evolving, learning, and expanding. The reset mindset invites us to remain open to the unknown, to the new lessons, opportunities, and passions that await us.

Consider Mark, who, in his mid-50s, decided to go back to school to pursue a long-held dream of becoming a writer. Many people, at his age, would have considered this a late or impractical decision, but Mark embraced the mindset of lifelong learning. He realized that it was never too late to chase what brought him joy and fulfillment. Along the way, he faced doubts, challenges, and fears, but he also experienced the exhilarating joy of starting something new and watching his writing evolve. Today, Mark is not only a published author but also a mentor to aspiring writers, encouraging them to pursue their passions no matter their age.

Mark's story exemplifies the spirit of lifelong growth. By embracing the reset mindset, we free ourselves from the constraints of age, circumstance, or past mistakes. We become open to the possibility of constant reinvention, knowing that our potential is not limited by where we've been, but rather by where we are willing to go.

The reset mindset encourages us to approach life with curiosity and wonder. It invites us to set new goals, explore new passions, and constantly reassess who we are becoming. Through this mindset, we learn that growth is not a linear path but a spiral, constantly expanding and deepening as we move through life's phases.

Conclusion

Living and thriving with a reset mindset is about choosing transformation, even in the face of adversity. It's about recognizing that the power to change lies within us, and that through courage, resilience, and connection, we can achieve a life filled with purpose, fulfillment, and joy. The journey is ongoing, but with each step, we learn more about who we are and what we are capable of. We grow not just for ourselves, but in service to the world around us. With a reset mindset, we not only survive the challenges life presents—we thrive.